Rosie Goes Home

Story by Pamela Rushby

Illustrations by Paul Könye

Contents

Chapter 1

Jack's Turn

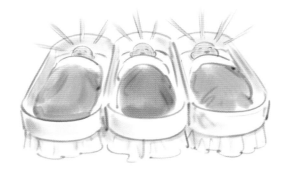

Rosie the parrot was being taken to Jack's apartment. Rosie made too much noise at Lee's place.

But when the children pushed the pram and Rosie's cage up to Jack's apartment, there seemed to be just as much noise there. From out in the hall, the children could hear crying.

"Who's crying?" asked Grace.

"My sisters," Jack said gloomily. "You knew my mum was going to have a baby? Well, she had three girls – triplets!"

"Three girls! That's wonderful!" Grace said.

"It's not wonderful," Jack said. "They never seem to be asleep at the same time. If one of them's asleep, the other two are crying!"

Jack's mum opened the door. She had a baby over her shoulder. The baby was crying loudly. "Come in!" Jack's mum said. "Is this Rosie? She's beautiful!"

"I hope Rosie won't be too noisy," Ahmed said.

Jack's mum laughed. "We won't even notice her. With Daisy, Poppy and Violet, what's one more noisy girl?"

"Waaaah!" the babies cried.

Rosie looked around her. "Cup of tea?" she squawked faintly. "Bill?"

"Waaaah!" the babies cried again.

Rosie tucked her head under her good wing.

"Is she going to sleep?" asked Jack's mum.

"I think it's the crying," said Lee. "She doesn't like the babies' crying."

"I'm afraid I can't stop them," Jack's mum said. "Babies do cry."

"Why don't you put Rosie in your room for a while, Jack?" Grace said.

"It's not my room any more," said Jack. "There's always a baby in it."

"I'm sorry, Jack," said his mum. "It's a small apartment, and if one of the babies is asleep I need to put her somewhere quiet. There's no one in your room, now, so let's have afternoon tea and see if Rosie will come out from under her wing."

"Okay," said Jack.

Chapter 2

Ahmed's Turn

The babies, Daisy, Poppy and Violet, took it in turns to cry all through afternoon tea. When the children looked in at Rosie, she had her head even further under her wing.

"It's no good," Lee said. "Rosie doesn't like the crying."

"I'm sorry, Jack," his mum said. "Maybe Rosie will be happier somewhere else."

"Then it's my turn!" said Ahmed.

Jack wasn't happy, but he could see Rosie was miserable in his apartment. He helped Ahmed put Rosie's cage back in the pram, and the children headed off to Ahmed's apartment.

"What's this?" Ahmed's mum said. "I thought we weren't having Rosie for a few days yet."

"Jack can't have her," Ahmed said. "So I can keep her for four days!"

"Well, I don't know," said Ahmed's mum. "Does it take much time to look after her? You have homework to do, you know. School is important."

"She doesn't take much time," Grace told Ahmed's mum.

Ahmed's younger brother, Jamil, thought Rosie was beautiful. He wanted to know all about parrots.

"We'll go to the library and get some books," Ahmed's mum said.

Chapter 3

Rosie's Adventure

The next morning, when the children went to school, Ahmed wasn't happy.

"It's Jamil," he said. "He wants to take Rosie to school to tell his whole class about parrots."

"That's all right, isn't it?" Grace said. "I took Rosie to school."

"It's all right as long as Mr Grimm doesn't see her," Ahmed said. "He's been doing a lot of work in the garden at the front. He's there all the time."

Sure enough, Mr Grimm was working in the garden on the day that Jamil took Rosie to school. The children stopped in the doorway with the pram. Grace tucked the blanket tightly around Rosie's cage, and Ahmed pushed the pram past Mr Grimm.

"Taking the baby for a walk, eh?" Mr Grimm said. "That's good!"

Then it happened. Jamil tried to tuck the blanket in tighter, but a wheel of the pram slipped off the path. Jamil grabbed at Rosie's cage to stop it falling, and the cage door sprang open.

There was a flash of red and blue and green and yellow as Rosie burst out of the cage. She couldn't fly very well, because her wing wasn't quite better. But she could fly well enough to land in a tree high above the children.

"Oh, no!" they all shouted.

Mr Grimm turned around. "What's going on?" he said.

Rosie flew off again, towards the park. The children ran after her.

"She's got out! Rosie's got out!" they shouted.

"Who's got out? Not the baby? What's going on?" Mr Grimm ran after them.

In the park, Rosie sat high in a tree. "How can we catch her?" Grace cried.

"We can't climb up there! Will she come back to the cage?" said Jack, holding it up.

Chapter 4

Chipper

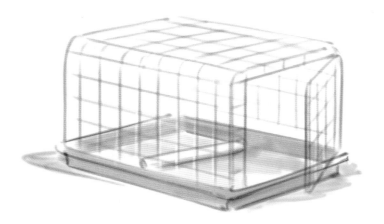

Mr Grimm ran over to the children. He looked at the pram and at the empty cage, then up into the tree. "Well, well!" he said. "So that's what's going on!"

Now the children didn't care if Mr Grimm knew about Rosie or not. "We can't get her back!" they cried.

"I think I can," said Mr Grimm. He held his hand up and called, "Chipper! Chipper! Come on, Chipper!"

Rosie looked down at Mr Grimm and flew straight onto his hand. She walked up his arm and put her head against his face. "Bill? Bill? Bill?" Rosie screeched. "Cup of tea, Bill?"

The children stared. Mr Grimm looked back at them.

"Why does she keep saying 'Bill'?" Jamil asked.

"Well, that's my name," said Mr Grimm. "Bill is short for William."

"Rosie's yours?" Grace said. "You've got a pet!"

Mr Grimm looked embarrassed. "Yes," he said.

"Mr Grimm!" said Jack. "A pet! But you know what the rules are!"

Mr Grimm looked even more embarrassed. "Yes, I do," he said. "No ball games, no bikes, no rollerblades. . ."

"And especially, no pets!" the children said.

"Well. . . perhaps pets are allowed," said Mr Grimm.

"Cup of tea?" squawked Rosie. "Bill?"